BITCOIN

Unlock the Secret World of Bitcoin

Bitcoin Wallet, Bitcoin Mining, Bitcoin Trading, Bitcoin Hard Fork, Satoshi Nakamoto, Blockchain Technology, Cryptocurrency

New Edition

By Kerry Gan

Disclaimer

All information and data in this book is for informational purpose only. I make no representations as to accuracy, completeness, suitability, or validity, of any information. I will not be liable for any errors, omissions, or any losses, injuries, or damages arising from its display or use.

Because the information in this book is based on my personal opinion and experience, it should not consider professional financial investment advice. The ideas and strategies should never be used without first assessing your own personal and financial situation, or without consulting a financial professional.

My thoughts and opinions will also change from time to time, as I learn and accumulate more knowledge. In any event, I'm not providing any Services (including but not limited to advisory services) relating to any securities in any jurisdiction.

Table of Contents

Introduction

Although bitcoin has gained global recognition and is rapidly being implemented across several various industries including healthcare, finance, real estate and much more, only a seemingly insignificant percentage of the population (when compared with the world population) has an understanding of the technology behind bitcoin and how to make the most of it.

A significant contributing factor to this seeming lack of knowledge is the fact that most people have the preconceived mindset that bitcoin is very technical and challenging to understand (somewhere in the category of rocket science).

This book seeks to simplify the bitcoin concept and demystify what would normally be perceived as "technical" or "complex". After going through the content of this book, readers will have an in-depth understanding of Bitcoin and can finally make informed decisions about the cryptocurrency.

What Is Bitcoin?

Bitcoin is typically regarded as a decentralized digital currency. Some Bitcoin holders have adopted the use of Bitcoin to pay for services.

Interestingly, several online services accept Bitcoin in place of fiat currencies.

Although its use was initially met with several challenges and restrictions, some leading stores and international companies now accept Bitcoin as payment, including Overstock and Microsoft, amongst others.

Additionally, a significant number of VPN and hosting websites accept Bitcoin.

On the other hand, because Bitcoin is decentralized and equally anonymous, some "dark" sites use Bitcoin in place of fiat currency.

The inconspicuousness and decentralization mean Bitcoin is ideal for situations where regular banking will pose a threat.

A feature that distinguishes bitcoin from regular fiat currency is the absence of a regulatory 'body' to produce and control the flow of the money. Primarily,

Bitcoin is maintained by users interconnected by a central ledger.

This ledger is made functional by what is called a blockchain. This blockchain documents every transaction made using Bitcoin, authorizes transactions, and ensures the integrity of the bitcoin network.

Bitcoin has since transformed from being the mysterious digital currency into being a necessary commodity. It is important to note that Bitcoins trade in decimal places, which implies that you can start using the crypto token without buying an entire Bitcoin.

One Bitcoin can cost as much as ten thousand dollars, a price that many people might not be able to afford. Alternatively, users can buy part of a Bitcoin.

For instance, if a user has about $1,000 and is looking to purchase Bitcoin, $1,000 Should buy about 0.11 BTC. Typically, If the price of Bitcoin rises, so does the amount the user has, and vice-versa when it falls.

5 Unique Features of Bitcoin

To give you a better understanding of Bitcoin, it is expedient that we point out some of how Bitcoin is different from conventional currencies. These features make Bitcoin such an authoritative possibility.

As expressed earlier, one of the main distinctions between Bitcoin and Fiat currencies is that Bitcoin is decentralized. It is hard for anyone to point to an individual, company, or government as the 'controller' of the Bitcoin network.

This, however, is not the only distinction there is, so with few points, let us examine some features that are restricted to Bitcoin, especially when compared with fiat currencies.

1. Bitcoin is not centralized.

It is common knowledge that conventional currency is usually controlled by a central authority - typically a section of the government. However, Bitcoin is decentralized.

Because it functions as a P-2-P (peer-to-peer) network, carrying out transactions and verifying these transactions are facilitated by various people in the network.

2. Bitcoin is a Computer-generated Currency.

Another feature that differentiates Bitcoin from conventional currency is the fact that it's computer-generated. Putting it simply, Bitcoin as a cryptocurrency exists in virtual space.

This implies that users cannot withdraw physical Bitcoin from the bank or an ATM. Although unauthorized physical depictions of bitcoins have been created by some people, everyone should note that Bitcoin is virtual.

3. Bitcoin is Scarce.

News has it that the amount of bitcoin to be created is currently capped at only 21 million bitcoins. Owing to this restriction, Bitcoin has the scarcity factor, unlike conventional currency that can be printed when governments decide to do so.

Interestingly, the amount of bitcoin generated from mining will half every four years to spread out the production of bitcoins being released into the market. What this means is that people will still be able to create them for about 100 years. Once the limit is reached, no new bitcoins will be generated, and the prevailing supply will enjoy the benefits of scarcity, making them more treasured.

4. Bitcoin transactions are irreversible.

To ensure that the blockchain of all bitcoin transactions is in chronological order, Bitcoin transactions typically irreversible. Furthermore, a Bitcoin transaction might take about fifteen minutes or more to confirm.

This is different from fiat currencies that characteristically process transactions in seconds and allow for reversing transactions made with them.

5. Bitcoin is not accepted in every country.

Anywhere in the world, it is expected that you will find local currencies. In most locations, you'll be able to exchange your country's money for the currency of the country you're visiting.

You'll also find out that no matter where you are in the world, you will be able to trade your fiat currency for goods and services. On the other hand, Bitcoin has not been embraced by the world at large.

Stunning Bitcoin History Reveal

There's a lot of controversy surrounding the history of Bitcoin and even the brain behind it-Satoshi Nakamoto. - Some people believe that Satoshi Nakamoto is an individual who used to live in Japan- and is already dead, some others accept that Nakamoto may be a shared pseudonym for a group of people.

News has it that Satoshi Nakamoto started working on the Bitcoin concept in 2007 (more than 10 years ago). On the 18th of August 2008, Bitcoin.org domain was officially registered anonymously.

This registration acted as an antecedent to the body of work that would describe the workings of the Bitcoin protocol (The Bitcoin whitepaper, which was released months later).

On October 31, 2008, Satoshi published a revolutionary white paper and went on to distribute it in a mailing list for cryptographers in November 2008. The white paper had about 9 (nine) pages and was called "Bitcoin - A peer-to-peer electronic cash system."

On the 3rd of January 2009, the founding block of

the Bitcoin blockchain-The Genesis block- was built successfully by Satoshi. Subsequently, the resultant Bitcoin software and the total amount of BTC created from being hardcoded with the Genesis block (50) could not be expended.

While we cannot say that this was precisely what Satoshi wanted to accomplish, there is always the possibility that it could have been a mistake. Whatever the case may be, it is another mystery to augment the Bitcoin story.

It was about six (6) days after the first block was created before the next block was added (thankfully, the time required has been drastically reduced to the 10 minutes that is valid presently). Concepts have been put forward to clarify the time frame for the first blockchain to exist.

While some say that Satoshi was mining the first block to test-run his network, other people have explained that the six days wait period was in a symbolic representation of the book of Genesis from the Bible, in which God created the world in six days.

The first-ever Bitcoin transaction took happened on the 12th of January 2009. This transaction was carried out between Nakamoto and an early contributor to the Bitcoin project-Hal Finney (although he is late now). News has it that Nakamoto sent 10 BTC to Hal Finney as a test, and the new computer scientist started mining blocks for himself.

October 5th, 2009 is an unforgettable date in the Bitcoin history as that was when the New Liberty Standard established the first-ever Bitcoin exchange rate against the dollar. As at then, $1 was equal to 2300.03 BTC.

On the 22nd of May 2010, the entire bitcoin community was astonished when the Bitcoin was used to buy physical merchandise. Laszlo Hanyecz offered Bitcoin users a platform on Bitcointalk.org to exchange BTC for Two Pizzas, and Jeremy Sturdivant bought two boxes of Pizza for 10,000 BTC. The famous Pizza bought by Jeremy Sturdivant was from Papa John's.

Even though the product purchased seems unimportant, it presented a massive Breakthrough for Bitcoin's placement as a cryptocurrency and its societal acceptance. Thankfully, Bitcoin has come a long way from being good for just pizza to enabling key transactions around the world.

On the 9th of February 2011, Bitcoin enjoyed a smooth ride to the top as it gained sameness with the US dollar at a 1:1 ratio, and still plying the upward route, Bitcoin skyrocketed from $1 to $31.91 in the space of just four months.

Nevertheless, only four days after the rise in price, on

June 12, 2011, Bitcoin drastically plunged in value to $10.25, which is now known in history as the first significant correction experienced by the Bitcoin community.

This drop in the value of Bitcoin also worsened with the occurrence of the major security breach of Mt. Goxon June 19, 2011.

In what seemed like a never-ending tale of woes, the price of bitcoin plunged more in-depth 6 months later when a famous e-wallet company announced that they would no longer be allowing BTC trading.

This time, a second major correction was experienced by the Bitcoin community, due to high volatility.

Moving back to positive Bitcoin news, in January 2015, Coinbase pulled 75 million USD as part of a funding round, smashing existing records for any bitcoin company.

By February 2015, Bitcoin's price climbed the ladder to reach $262. By March, 21 Inc-a Bitcoin start-up-made it public that it had raised 116 million USD for venture funding.

A standard set of rules was maintained by users of the Bitcoin until the 1st of August 2017, where bitcoin split into the bitcoin (BTC) chain with 1 MB block size limit and the Bitcoin Cash (BCH) chain with 8 MB block size limit.

It is also worth mentioning that just less than one year after the collapse of Mt.Gox, United Kingdom-based exchange Bitstamp publicized that they would be taking their exchange offline to provide for the examination of a hack which resulted in the theft of over 19,000 bitcoins from their wallet.

The exchange was offline for several days, with users hypothesizing that their funds had been lost. Nevertheless, Bitstamp resumed trading on the 9th of January after they enhanced security measures and assured customers that their account balances would not be changed.

On the 6th of December 2017, Steam- A software marketplace- publicized that it would no longer accept bitcoin as payment for its products, referring to slow transactions' speeds, price volatility, and high fees for transactions as reasons for their decision.

6 Benefits of Bitcoin

• Independence: Bitcoin users can send and receive Bitcoins anywhere in the world, regardless of local currency.

• Users are in charge: There is no central body to control new Bitcoin. As we have explained earlier, new coins are mined by user's computers, indicating that the users are in control of the network.

• Bitcoin is Transparent: The blockchain ledger sustaining Bitcoin is available to anyone who wants to have it. Several sites allow users to verify transactions, while private information remains concealed.

• Privacy: Although ways abound to trace Bitcoin transactions back to their source, Bitcoin is chiefly anonymous.

Along with confidentiality, Bitcoin transactions are protected against identity theft and credit/debit card fraud by making use of only digital wallet IDs, and not the actual details of the users.

• Scarcity: There is a limited supply of Bitcoin; by now, you already know that the total amount of bitcoin to be made available to the users is only about 21 million Bitcoin.

Several million are previously alleged to be irreversibly lost, fueling the demand for the available ones. For now, Bitcoin is the standard almost all other cryptocurrencies measure against.

• Security: Notwithstanding the scams available for unscrupulous people to sell fake Bitcoins, users can be assured that no one can fake a Bitcoin.

Is Bitcoin really anonymous?

Bitcoin is often called anonymous because users can send and receive bitcoins without having to provide any information that reveals their identities.

In the early days of Bitcoin, its users assumed that their transactions could not be traced to the blockchain. However, as time passed, it was discovered that Bitcoin being a public blockchain made bitcoin transactions open for all to see.

Attaining practical anonymity with Bitcoin can be complicated, and achieving absolute anonymity may be unattainable.

Sending and receiving bitcoins can be likened to performing using a pseudonym. If a performer's alias is ever connected with their identity, all they did under that pseudonym will now be linked to them.

In Bitcoin, the address to which you receive Bitcoin is regarded as your pseudonym. All transactions related to that address is deposited forever in the blockchain. Therefore, if your address is ever linked to your identity, all transactions will be linked to you.

It was recommended in the original Bitcoin whitepaper that Bitcoin users employ a new address for each transaction to prevent the transactions being linked to a single owner.

This would be the equivalent of doing different performances under different pseudonyms. Though this can be described as a good practice, it is not enough to ensure full anonymity.

Hard Fork VS Soft Fork

The decentralized nature of Bitcoin is such that participants on the bitcoin network are required to reach an agreement regarding the shared state of the blockchain.

Full consensus amongst network participants brings about a single blockchain of verified data that everyone considers as correct. Typically, a blockchain fork will occur when there is a departure from consensus.

There are two main types of programming fork: hard and soft.

Hard Fork

A hard fork is a modification to a protocol that makes older versions invalid. If older versions keep running, these versions will end up with a different protocol and with diverse data than the newer version. This can cause substantial confusion and likely error.

With bitcoin, a hard fork would be needed to alter crucial factors, which include the size of the block, the complexity of the cryptographic puzzle that should be solved, restrictions to other information that can be added, and so on. An alteration to any of these factors would trigger blocks to be recognized by the new protocol but banned by older versions and could cause serious problems – perhaps even a loss of funds.

For instance, if the block size limit were to be moved from 2MB to 5MB, a 4MB block would be recognized by nodes running the new version but banned by nodes running the older version.

To paint a clearer picture, try to imagine that the 4MB block is authenticated by an updated node and added on to the blockchain.

If the next block is verified by a node running an older version of the protocol, it will try to add its block to the blockchain, but then will spot that the latest block is not valid.

Consequently, this node will disregard that block and ascribe its new authentication to the previous one.

Unexpectedly, two blockchains emerge, one with a combination of older and newer version blocks, and another with only older version blocks. The fastest-growing chain will hinge on which nodes validate the next blocks. The two chains may extend in parallel indefinitely.

A hard fork has a huge tendency to be messy. It is also hazardous, as it opens the possibility that bitcoins expended in a new block could then be spent again on an old block.

The available solution is for one division to be abandoned in favor of the other, which entails that some miners will lose out even though the transactions would not be lost but would rather just be re-allocated.

Another solution is for all nodes to switch to the newer version at the same time, although this might be difficult to accomplish in a distributed, widely spread system.

Soft Fork

A soft fork is described as a backward well-suited technique of upgrading a blockchain. Putting it simply, a soft fork is a software upgrade that is compatible with older versions of the software.

Soft forks do not require nodes on the network to upgrade for them to maintain consensus because all blocks on the soft-forked blockchain track the old set of consensus rules as well as the new ones.

Nevertheless, blocks formed by nodes meeting the requirements of the old set of consensus rules will violate the new set of consensus rules, and as a result, will perhaps be made redundant by the advancing mining majority.

This is because, for a soft fork to work, most miners need to be aware of and implement the new set of consensus rules. If this majority is reached, then the older network will no longer be used, with the newer blockchain gaining recognition as the real blockchain.

An instance of a soft fork is the use of a new rule changing the network block size from 4MB to 1MB. Nodes that have not upgraded will keep seeing incoming transactions as valid, as these nodes adhere to the old set of consensus rules as well as the new.

Nevertheless, mining nodes that have not upgraded and try to mine new blocks will have these blocks rejected, as it does not correspond with the new set of consensus guidelines (block sizes of 1MB).

Consequently, the blockchain with 4MB sized blocks is expected to fall into neglect as miners enforce the new consensus rule of 1MB.

Hot Wallet VS Cold Wallet

A cryptocurrency wallet is a way of storing cryptocurrency.

You should note that a wallet does not house cryptocurrency tokens in the same way that a normal wallet does for your money.

Users can't procure Bitcoin and put them in their wallets, but they can get Bitcoin and hold them securely using their wallets. Two types of wallets exist; the hot and cold wallet.

What is a hot wallet?

A hot wallet is utilized online through platforms that proffer Bitcoin storage services.

When hot wallets are used, the user hands over their private and public keys to the platform, which then oversees and secures both keys.

It is not advisable to leave large amounts of Bitcoin in a hot wallet as the systems could be susceptible to hacking.

It is also recommended that you carry out thorough research into the wallet provider before signing up as there are wicked scam platforms that are always trying to steal funds from helpless users.

Usually, hot wallets are simpler to set up, use, and take more tokens. But then again, hot wallets are also more vulnerable to hackers, likely regulation, and other procedural weaknesses.

What is a cold wallet?

A cold wallet is entirely offline. Usually, a cold wallet can be presented in software forms, including applications that are operated on a computer or smartphone, or as a hardware device, which is worked in but stays offline.

Cold hardware wallets are deemed the most reliable method of keeping your Bitcoin safely stored. Generally, cold wallets are more secure, but they don't admit as many Bitcoins as many of the hot wallets.

5 Ways to Get Bitcoins

There are several ways to get Bitcoin. Users can buy a significant number of bitcoins online, in person, or slowly receive a substantial amount of bitcoins for free by playing mobile or online games, completing tasks on websites, or writing about cryptocurrency.

1. Get Bitcoin with Affiliate Marketing for FREE

Affiliate marketing is a popular way to earn money for both social media influencers and everyday people to get Bitcoin for FREE.

Businesses provide particular URLs or codes for influencers (or affiliate marketers) to send out to their audiences.

If somebody clicks on that link and makes a purchase on your affiliate link, you will receive a Bitcoin reward.

2. Get Paid in Bitcoin

To get Bitcoin, it is a great idea to accept Bitcoin as payment for your work. This is a particularly attractive option if you want to earn bitcoin from home or through freelancing.

Irrespective of your career path or the type of service

you offer, it is possible for you to money with cryptocurrency in exchange for your services now.

3. Earn Bitcoin by Trading or Mining

For most crypto enthusiasts, trading Bitcoin is the easiest way for them to get more Bitcoin.

There are quite a lot of trading approaches, and every trader has their selected way to increase their crypto holdings through trading.

Nevertheless, a progressively popular way for users to trade is by leverage trading.

4. Buy Bitcoins

If you'd prefer to buy bitcoins, you can choose to use websites to help you find a Bitcoin ATM, which functions in the same way as a regular ATM, only that with this, you trade your cash for Bitcoin.

Alternatively, there are a couple of retail stores across the United States that will give you Bitcoin in exchange for cash.

Websites also exist to help you find bank branches that will give you bitcoin in exchange for cash deposits. You can also get bitcoins directly on exchange platforms that exist to match buyers with sellers.

5. Bitcoin Mining

Bitcoin mining is the management of transactions in the digital currency system, in which the accounts of existing Bitcoin transactions, known as blocks, are appended to the record of past transactions, known as the blockchain.

Miners use software that makes use of their processing capacity to resolve transaction-related algorithms. Subsequently, they are awarded a certain number of Bitcoins per block.

Trading Costs that MUST BE AWARE

If you are looking to buy and sell bitcoin on an exchange, you should be aware that some fees apply to trading.

Most exchanges charge deposit fees, trading fees, and withdrawal fees. It is important to note that these fees can have a significant impact on the overall cost of your Bitcoin trades.

Also, it should be put into consideration that Bitcoin exchange fees can also differ from one account to the next, with some users able to unlock reduced costs because of several factors, which include Account verification, Trading volume, and Length of membership.

Exchanges charge between 0.1-0.25% as maker and taker fees.

You are required to pay maker fees when your order is not instantly tallied against a trade already on the exchange's order book. What this means is that you are giving more liquidity to the order book, so most exchanges will repay you with lower fees.

On the other hand, taker fees are necessary for trades that are implemented against other trades that already exist in the exchange's order book. This eliminates liquidity from the market. Consequently, taker fees are typically higher than maker fees.

5 real-life applications for Bitcoin

You might want to understand the real-life implications of Bitcoin, and how the digital currency is transforming things in the lives of real people. Here are some scenarios of how Bitcoin can be used:

• Bitcoin can be used as a store of value which is like having a bank account

• Bitcoin can also be used for shopping purposes. Bitpay is a popular shopping app that allows users to spend Bitcoin in exchange for regular stuff.

• A lot of people buy Bitcoin as an investment. Coinbase is a famous coin exchange people use to invest in Bitcoin. Interestingly, those who started the investment journey early and dared to stay the course have been handsomely rewarded. Bitcoin has pulled up a return over 50,000%, something that no other investment has been able to match.

• Bitcoin allows you to send value across the world faster and with lower fees compared to banks and other financial institutions.

Real estate is another area where bitcoin is receiving impressive acceptance. Interestingly, Southern California company Glen Oaks Escrow announced in

2018 that it will start accepting payment in Bitcoin and Bitcoin Cash through BitPay.

Glen Oaks reported in their official release that the decision to start accepting BTC as payment came about as a result of the rising number of properties being sold for BTC, referring to a home in Lake Tahoe that sold for 2,739 BTC, the equivalent of USD 1.6M at the time. A luxury home in Houston, Texas, listed on their website sold for 74.18 BTC (1,099,000 USD).

Is Bitcoin Safe to Use?

In the times past, the right use and appropriate storage of Bitcoin have established that the crypto token is a consistent financial tool when it comes to storing value, fortifying distributed person-to-person cash transfers, and openness.

The underlying technology behind Bitcoin is robust enough to keep back the most hi-tech strikes. To be honest, a large percentage of unsettling stories around Bitcoin hacks are owing to the negligence of external service providers or critical mishandling.

Therefore, it is safe to say that when all the guidelines are followed to the letter, Bitcoin is secure to use.

Nevertheless, as applies to every other type of currency, there are some matters Bitcoin users should be aware of to guard their monies.

These include Bitcoin price instability, safe storage of cryptocurrency, use of uncertain external services, and data security issues.

Bitcoin Alternatives – Altcoins

The world-wide favorable reception of bitcoin has given rise to the launch of more than a few crypto tokens trying to break its record.

This is probably possible because bitcoin has always been an open-source project, and virtually everyone with an internet connection holds the license to create their solutions off the unique bitcoin project.

Bitcoin alternatives are generally referred to as Altcoins. Altcoins are the alternative cryptocurrencies revealed after the global acceptance of Bitcoin. Typically, these altcoins are presented by their developers as improved replacements for Bitcoin.

We can all agree that the success of Bitcoin as the pioneer peer-to-peer digital currency set the pace for Altcoins to follow. Quite a lot of altcoins seek to solve the apparent limitations linked with bitcoins and to build up new solutions with competitive advantages.

The growth of these Bitcoin alternatives is an encouraging sign of the growth of decentralized technologies.

The first Altcoin was launched in 2011, two years after Bitcoin's first launch in 2009. Namecoin was the first Altcoin to be launched. Its launch also made way for the birth of altcoins, as a few altcoins were launched following its release.

Although the first altcoin was launched in 2011, the regularity of altcoin launches increased exponentially in 2013, and presently, there is an altcoin launch every other week, causing the total number of altcoins launched to be an estimated 2500-3000.

We should note that some of the launched altcoins were just announced and had their codes released without their genesis block being created. Some poorly schemed altcoins have been unveiled but did not stay around for long before going into extinction.

Several Bitcoin alternatives have a lot of characteristics that can be associated with Bitcoin. And some of them include Ethereum, Litecoin, Ripple, EOS, Dash, and so on.

Ethereum: Ethereum is an open-source, blockchain-based distributed computing platform and operating system with a smart contract functionality.

It presents a modified version of the Bitcoin consensus through transaction-based state transitions. The token whose blockchain is generated by the Ethereum platform is referred to as Ether.

Ethereum also presents a decentralized software

platform that enables smart contracts and distributed applications to be built and run without any downtime, fraud, control, or interference from a third party.

Litecoin: Litecoin (LTC) is an altcoin and an open-source project that was unveiled in 2017, and as expected, it was born out of Bitcoin's existence and shared a lot of technical functions with the cryptocurrency.

The first idea backing the Litecoin project was the necessity to develop a quicker and low-priced token to use as a substitute to Bitcoin.

In other words, Litecoin was designed to allow faster and cheaper blockchain-based transactions.

Ripple: The fantastic fact about Ripple is that it acts as both a crypto platform and an alternative to Bitcoin, the ripple platform was established to permit high-speed and cheap transactions.

Like Bitcoin, it is an open-source platform. The platform has its currency (XRP) but also allows everybody to use the platform to create their own via their website.

Conclusion

Bitcoin is a decentralized digital currency that is being used to pay for goods and services.

Apart from being decentralized, Bitcoin is also virtual, immutable, transparent, and secure. It is important to note that your bitcoin being anonymous is purely hinged on your ability to keep your public or private key from being linked to you.

While you can carry out transactions with your pseudonym (public/private key), the transaction can be traced back to you if the key is traced to you.

There are several ways to get Bitcoin. Users can buy a significant number of bitcoins online, in person, or slowly receive a substantial amount of bitcoins for free by playing mobile or online games, completing tasks on websites, or writing about cryptocurrency. When you choose to buy Bitcoin, you can decide to do so OTC (over the counter), through an exchange, or in person.

Fees apply to trade Bitcoin. Most exchanges charge deposit fees, trading fees, and withdrawal fees. It is important to note that these fees can have a significant impact on the overall cost of your Bitcoin trades.

Also, it should be put into consideration that Bitcoin exchange fees can also differ from one account to the next, with some users able to unlock reduced costs because of several factors, which include Account verification, Trading volume, and Length of membership.

Exchanges charge between 0-2.5% as maker and taker fees and about 7% for instant buy.

Now you know all there is to know about Bitcoin. The choice to embrace this digital token or not solely rests with you.

Thank You

Thank you for reading! It's so amazing to see people reading my books. Like most writers, I used to think I wasn't good enough, so I didn't try. With the encouragement of my business partners, clients, friends, and family members, I was able to give this series a go. I'm eternally grateful for each reader enjoyed reading my books and put the books on their virtual shelf.

If you enjoyed this book or found it is useful, I'd be very grateful if you'd post a short review on Amazon. Your support does make a difference, and I read all the reviews personally so I can get your feedback and make the next book even better.

If you would like to explore more about cryptocurrency, make sure to check out my other crypto books on Amazon.

Once again, sincerely thank you for the support!

About The Author

Kerry Gan is an accomplished self-published author with more than a decade of experience in Forex, Binary Option, Blockchain, and Crypto industry by holding senior positions in multiple international financial and fintech institutions.

Kerry is an early investor for Litecoin back in 2014, a private investor for EOS and IOTA. He is the Blockchain Strategist from the University of Oxford, and founding member of the Association of Blockchain Development in Hong Kong.

Kerry holds a Master of Applied Finance from the University of Adelaide, and he is also a Certified Financial Planner (CFP©) for financial planning and wealth management.